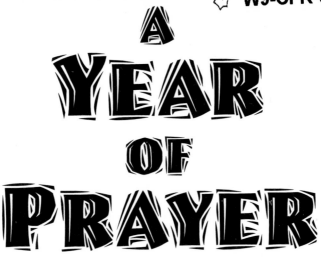

A YEAR OF PRAYER

JEANNE HINTON

Augsburg

A YEAR OF PRAYER
365 Reflections for Spiritual Growth

First North American edition published 1995 by Augsburg Fortress, Minneapolis
Copyright © 1995 Hunt & Thorpe, London, England
Text © *Jeanne Hinton*
Illustrations © *Sue Climpson, Jane Reynolds*
Designed by *Jim Weaver Design*

Scripture quotations are from the Holy Bible: New International Version, unless otherwise indicated in the text.

Library of Congress Cataloging-in-Publication Data

A year of prayer : 365 reflections for spiritual growth.
        p.   cm.
    ISBN 0-8066-2757-3 (alk. paper)
     1. Prayer—Christianity—Quotations, maxims, etc.   I. Augsburg
Fortress (Publisher)
   BV205.Y43   1995
   242'.2—dc20
                                      95-17188
                                        CIP

Printed and bound in Malaysia
                                      AF 9-2757
99 98 97 96 95 1 2 3 4 5 6 7 8 9 10

Introduction

Everyone prays. Sometimes we are not conscious of the fact that we are praying, or we would not call what we do "prayer." Nevertheless, it is likely that we pray – in one way or another – most of the time. Becoming aware of that fact is important.

Amy Carmichael beautifully sums up the essence of prayer: "Often in the throng of the day's work, there will not be time for more than a very little prayer – a thought, a touch, a feeling, a cry – but it is enough."

Prayer grows and deepens from the awareness that I am praying, as I allow the experience to deepen and grow in ways that are true for me. Each of us has a different and unique relationship with God; it takes on the color of who I am as well as who God is. This makes for an exciting adventure as I discover, not only more of God, but also more of myself.

Sometimes our prayers are not like this. Sometimes they are a form, a set of prayers – perhaps ones left over from our childhood. It may be that we have not discovered all that prayer can be for us as adults, and therefore we have not grown in our prayer lives.

In recent years there has been a good deal of research into ways that personality colors prayer and prayer enhances personality. We now understand more clearly why different forms of prayer come naturally to some and not to others. The use of imagination, of our bodies, of symbols, play, and creativity – all these are methods that can enhance our exploration of prayer. Because of our unique personalities, we will be more naturally drawn to some of these methods than to others. All are likely to be of help to us at some point; but some will be of particular value.

The other side to our uniqueness is the common humanity that we all share. We are different from each other, but not so different that we cannot learn from one another. This book draws on the experiences of many Christians who have written down the insights they gained in their own spiritual journeys.

Use this book slowly and reflectively over the days and months of one year. There is an introduction to each month's theme and a short reading for each day. You may choose to add a simple personal exercise in prayer on some or many of the days. As you read, note the selections that speak most meaningfully to you and those which stir curiosity or wonder. Spend time with those readings. Try to discover why you are drawn to them.

A book such as this can provide markers that confirm or open up directions in prayer. There are weightier books that can take you deeper. Sometimes, however, short readings can hit home better than longer or more weighty ones. This was true for me as I gathered the quotations, and I hope that it will be your experience as you set out on *A Year of Prayer*.

CONTENTS

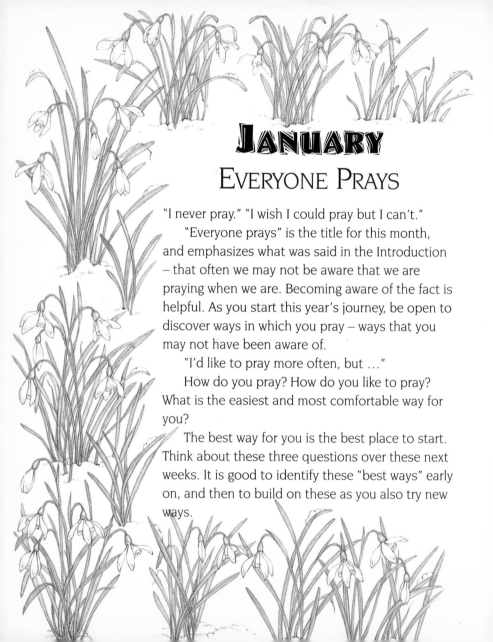

JANUARY

EVERYONE PRAYS

"I never pray." "I wish I could pray but I can't."

"Everyone prays" is the title for this month, and emphasizes what was said in the Introduction – that often we may not be aware that we are praying when we are. Becoming aware of the fact is helpful. As you start this year's journey, be open to discover ways in which you pray – ways that you may not have been aware of.

"I'd like to pray more often, but …"

How do you pray? How do you like to pray? What is the easiest and most comfortable way for you?

The best way for you is the best place to start. Think about these three questions over these next weeks. It is good to identify these "best ways" early on, and then to build on these as you also try new ways.

1

To wish to pray is a prayer in itself.

DIARY OF A COUNTRY PRIEST

2

Prayer is a way of thinning the clouds that dull our vision.

TILDEN EDWARDS

3

When you are overtired, burdened by responsibilities and cares, overwhelmed with work … forget yourself and stop for a moment; place everything in God's hands. This will require an act of faith, of adoration, and of love, and so you will already have laid the foundation for prayer.

MICHEL QUOIST

Prayer fastens the soul to God.

MONICA FURLONG

If thou dost love God, thou dost pray.

JULIAN OF NORWICH

There are many ways of praying, as there are many ways of expressing love. If people ask me how they should pray I throw the ball back with the question: "How do you like best to pray? How do you pray when you are at your best?" Your way is the best way for you.

WILLIAM JOHNSTON

If the only prayer you say in your whole life is "thank you," that would suffice.

MEISTER ECKHART

God gives prayer to the man who prays.

JOHN CLIMACUS

How do we detect the spark of religion within us? I imagine that it is different in each person, which would not be surprising since every person is unique. I think it has something to do with a longing deep within us.

BASIL HUME

10

Every time and every place is a time and place for prayer.

CATHERINE DE SIENA

11

He prays best who doesn't even know he's praying.

ST ANTHONY

12

Teach me to pray. Pray thyself in me.

FRANÇOIS FENELON

13

Sometimes we are very much disappointed with ourselves because we cannot pray proper prayers, only little ones that hardly seem to be prayers at all… Often in the throng of the day's work, there will not be time for more than a very little prayer – a thought, a touch, a feeling, a cry – but it is enough.

AMY CARMICHAEL

14

Pray as you can, not as you can't.

DOM CHAPMAN

15

The best prayers are often more groans than words.

JOHN BUNYAN

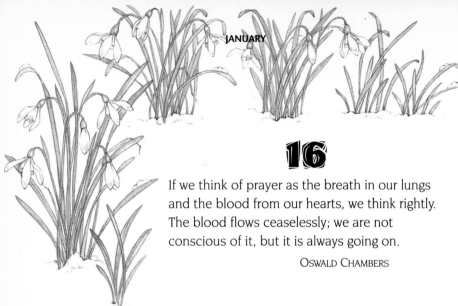

16

If we think of prayer as the breath in our lungs and the blood from our hearts, we think rightly. The blood flows ceaselessly; we are not conscious of it, but it is always going on.

OSWALD CHAMBERS

17

God is nearer to me than I am to myself; He is just as near to wood and stone, but they do not know it.

MEISTER ECKHART

18

Prayer then involves all things, and is an attempt to bring all things into focus, to see all things as they really are, as seen by God.

MELVYN MATTHEWS

19

Prayer is "the raising of the mind and heart to God."

LAURENCE FREEMAN

Every human soul has a certain latent capacity for God.

EVELYN UNDERHILL

To pray is to anchor the finite will in the will of God.

J H OLDHAM

22

Prayer is an essential part of a fully human life. If we do not pray we are only half alive and our faith is only half developed.

LAURENCE FREEMAN

23

Prayer is concerned with making meaningful all that has passed through (our) experience.

ALAN ECCLESTONE

Prayer is really our whole life toward God: our longing for Him, our "incurable God-sickness" as Barth calls it, our whole drive towards Him.

Evelyn Underhill

God wants us to pray and will tell us how to begin where we are.

The Cloud of Unknowing

Give us today our daily bread.

Lord's Prayer

Do not forget prayer. Every time you pray, if your prayer is sincere, there will be new feeling and new meaning in it, which will give you fresh courage.

Fyodor Dostoyevski

Prayer is the most personal act possible to man.

William McNamara

A man is what he prays.

ALAN ECCLESTONE

Prayer is the effort to live in the spirit of the whole.

SAMUEL COLERIDGE

31

Prayer is
The world in tune.

HENRY VAUGHAN

FEBRUARY

PRAYER IS USING MY IMAGINATION

"Imagination is a much neglected faculty," writes Gerard Hughes.

It is not that we do not use our imagination; often we wish our imagination was not so vivid. It conjures up all kinds of spectres. All of us imagine, dream, conjecture, some more than others. But do we value our imagination as a gift or faculty we can use – to help us pray, to solve problems, to release our creativity?

When Ignatius of Loyala was lying sick on his bed he began to daydream. Sometimes his dreams were of gaining great glory on the battlefield; at other times of enduring hardship in order to become a great saint. He became aware that his dreams about sainthood energized him, while the other daydreams caused him to feel depressed. This insight changed the course of his life, and led the way to his developing his "spiritual exercises" that continue today to teach us how to use our imagination prayerfully.

With the use of our imagination we can relive a scene in the gospels. We can become a part of that event, or we can return to places familiar to us, move into the future or take ourselves to some place far away. One such "imaginative journey" remains a clear memory. It was the day of Namibia's independence. I had prayed and worked for this together with others in this country. I would have loved to have been there in Namibia to join in the celebrations. I couldn't, so instead that day I spent an hour in prayer being present in my imagination – seeing, hearing, smelling, touching, talking. At the end I felt that I had been there and more that my life had been deeply touched by this imaginary encounter.

Another area that we often neglect is that of dreams. If we take the time to write down our dreams and to unravel their symbolism, they will yield valuable insights. The Bible tells of God speaking to people through their dreams; it is full of vivid symbolism and fantastic images. Again as Gerard Hughes says, "… images are much more likely to move us than words."

It is imagination that gives shape to the universe.

BARRY LOPEZ

While ... it was supposed that faith resides in the intelligence, it may be more realistic ... to say that faith resides in the imagination.

GREGORY BAUM

How does God speak to us? ... I pray ... Then he comes, and in his own gentle way, fills my mind with his thoughts and his vision.

JOHN POWELL

God has access to us through (the) power of imagination. I once discussed this avenue of God into us with a prayerful psychologist, and it was her opinion that there would always be "something surprising, distinctive and lasting" in the communication of God. I think she is right.

JOHN POWELL

Read of what has been done (in the Gospels) as though it were happening now … Offer yourself as present to what was said and done through our Lord Jesus Christ with the whole affective power of your mind … Hear and see these things being narrated as though you were hearing with your own ears and seeing with your own eyes.

LUDOLPH OF SAXONY

As I could not make reflection with my understanding I contrived to picture Christ within me. I did many simple things of this kind. I believe my soul gained very much in this way, because I began to practice prayer without knowing what it was.

TERESA OF AVILA

And whenever you read the Gospel, Christ Himself is speaking to you. And while you read, you are praying and talking with him.

TIKKON OF ZADONSK

By visualizations and by acting out it is possible to bring together the outer and inner in our daily living.

JAMES ROOSE-EVANS

Imagination and its expression in dreams, daydreams and fantasies are, I believe, an important part of what it is to be human. Imagination is an essential part of both human freedom and creativity. Thus it is bound up with our likeness of God.

LAWRENCE OSBORN

Imagination is a much neglected faculty. Images are much more likely to move us than words.

GERARD HUGHES

Symbols speak to us with all the subtlety and suggestiveness of great poetry … They hint. They point. They nudge … They thus call forth our own creativity, imagination and openness – precisely the faculties that enrich prayer.

CHARLES ELLIOTT

Night is a time of great wisdom, of great creativity, when powerful insights issue from the unconscious, either in dreams or during the twilight zone between sleeping and waking. And night is a time of problem-solving and of growth.

WILLIAM JOHNSTON

It may well be our imaginative capacity, which is always characterized by a sense of play, that really makes us human.

MORTON KELSEY

Imaginations differ; we need to let God use the one we have and not bemoan the one we do not have.

WILLIAM BARRY

Human beings need images, stories, myths, drama, song, colors, shapes, movements … when faced with realities that are beneath the surface of life.

CHRISTOPHER COELHO

16

Only mystics, clowns and artists, in my experience, speak the truth, which … imagination alone can grasp.

MALCOLM MUGGERIDGE

17

I know that this world is a world of imagination and vision.

WILLIAM BLAKE

18

It is only in exceptional moods that we realize how wonderful are the commonest experiences of life. It seems to me sometimes that these experiences have an "inner" side to them, as well as the outer side we normally perceive.

J W N SULLIVAN

19

Poetry, art, religion, ritual and celebration … We indulge in these activities not to achieve something but because unconsciously we feel the need to touch the roots of our being and of our common humanity.

CHRISTOPHER COELHO

Symbols of our inner truth may be images, happenings, objects or sounds; they may be noticed in dreams, in art forms or in the most ordinary experience. Whatever their form, they express a profound meaning that is beyond the grasp of words.

CAROLE MARIE KELLY

Our image of God, the kind of God we believe in, is to my mind crucial to the way our journey of prayer proceeds.

PHILIP SHELDRAKE

22

Images of God and self are very closely connected, and a change in one brings about a change in the other.

KATHLEEN FISCHER

23

Praying for others depends upon their being real for me, and those closest to me are naturally the most real. But other people can become real to me by the use of my imagination.

H A WILLIAMS

24

What our imagination can do for individuals, it can also sometimes do for whole peoples and cultures.

H A WILLIAMS

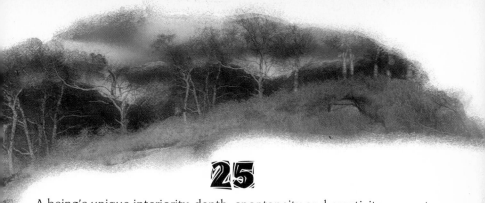

25

A being's unique interiority, depth, spontaneity and creativity present the creative unfolding and ultimate mystery of the cosmos.

CHARLENE SPRETNAK

26

Ritual, art, and story can make the world better, more just, and more whole. As we see our lives in words, images, and music, our hopes are raised and we become energized.

JAMES CONLON

27

Every person needs to learn to trust his or her own images.

MATTHEW FOX

28

You must give birth to your images. They are the future waiting to be born.

RAINER MARIA RILKE

MARCH

PRAYER IS BEING EXPRESSIVE

Praise (God) with the sounding of the trumpet;
praise him with harp and lyre. Praise him with
tambourine and dancing; praise him with the
strings and flute. Praise him with the clash of
cymbals, praise him with resounding cymbals.
Psalm 150:3-5

    Ancient Hebrew worship was full of noise
and color. Such vitality is found in Christian

worship in many cultures today. In others it is more muted, formal. But if we are to be fully ourselves before God, there will be times when a loud shout or an ecstatic dance will be what we most feel like doing. Then do it we should. Such an act may not always be appropriate in public worship, but on our own or with friends; why not? God will be delighted!

There are other forms of expression that are equally important. Our love for God resides deep within. Words are often inadequate, unless words are our stock in trade. Through different art forms we express ourselves with paint or wood or clay or wool; in this way what is deep within becomes more apparent not least to ourselves. It is part of the journey God is leading us on – to know God's image in us.

Walking, cycling, gardening, swimming, running – all the active sports and hobbies – how are these prayer? They help prayer in that they bring a balance, a rhythm to our lives that is essential to going deeper in prayer. But they can be prayer too. "I'm just talking a walk with God." To do it with that awareness becomes prayer. Indeed, are we not all the time "with God" in our various activities; prayer is the awareness of that fact.

The body is good, listen to what it tells you.

THOMAS MERTON

The artist is no more and no less than a contemplative who has learned to express himself, and who tells his love in color, speech, or sound.

EVELYN UNDERHILL

God respects me when I work, but he loves me when I sing.

RABINDRANATH TAGORE

At the same moment the Trinity filled me with heartfelt joy …
Benedicite Domine I said, and I meant it in all reverence, even though
I said it at the top of my voice.

JULIAN OF NORWICH

See meditation and prayer as
holistic – as activities of the
whole person. Raise to God
not only your mind and heart
but also your body and your
breathing, your bones and
your blood, your head and
your hands and your feet.
Keep nothing back from God.
Your whole life belongs to
him. Love God not with part
of your being but with your
whole being.

WILLIAM JOHNSTON

Prayer is a spontaneous cry of the heart, sometimes in jubilant exultation, sometimes poignant anguish, often in the stunned silence of adoration or the transforming union of love.

WILLIAM MCNAMARA

The Christian at prayer, therefore, does not always sit in a serene and tranquil posture of stillness and receptivity. Sometimes he pounds his fists on the wall or paces the floor: sometimes like Job he argues with God, or, like Jacob, wrestles with him and comes out maimed for life; sometimes he dances joyfully like David in the Lord's presence.

CLIFFORD LONGLEY

Our substance and our sensuality together are rightly named our soul.

JULIAN OF NORWICH

Pay attention to your body. It is a tangible expression of your life.

TILDEN EDWARDS

Our bodies are our bridge to the world, as we are in our bodies, so will we be in the world. More than that, we will be in eternity, for the road to the sacred runs through the carnal.

KENNETH LEECH

(Contemplation) is … life itself, fully awake, fully active, fully aware that it is alive. It is spiritual wonder. It is spontaneous awe at the sacredness of life, of being.

THOMAS MERTON

For to be a saint is, in a sense, to become more intensely ordinary, more deeply human, more passionate.

KENNETH LEECH

We should think of our senses as gifts of God and antennas of learning. In fact, one of the laws of learning is that the more senses are involved in the learning process, the deeper the lessons will penetrate and the longer they will be remembered.

JOHN POWELL

14

I began to listen to myself. Not to my inner chatter and judgment but to my inner music. I spent hours in sound and silence. I began to realize how these simple, powerful tools of breath and sound alter blood flow, skin temperature and stress.

DON CAMPBELL

15

Touching is an important form of communication. At times the slightest touch can say something, can express a warmth that words cannot convey.

JOHN POWELL

16

Have your feelings, own them and express them, and above all learn from them.

JOHN POWELL

17

Gardening is an active participation in the deepest mysteries of the universe.

THOMAS BERRY

18

To be truly *homo religiosus* (a religious person), one must bring together the outside and the inside, finding God both "out there" and "in here".

JAMES ROOSE-EVANS

19

Pay attention to your movement.

TILDEN EDWARDS

20

Walking can be a wonderfully contemplative exercise.

WILLIAM JOHNSTON

21

There is a necessity for movement when words are inadequate. The basis of all dancing is something deep within you.

MARTHA GRAHAM

22

The act of poetry is being aware of one's destiny and of the will of God.

CAITLIN MATTHEWS

23

I've also discovered an edge of holy sanity in the madness of competitive sports. When I have a team to support, then I seem more capable of really getting involved, energized, alert, present … A clear opportunity for meditation, for simple presence, for a playful window, can be found in participative sports.

TILDEN EDWARDS

24

Art enables us to find ourselves and lose ourselves at the same time. The mind that responds to the intellectual and spiritual values that lie hidden in a poem, a painting, or a piece of music, discovers a spiritual vitality that lifts it above itself, takes it out of itself, and makes it present to itself on a level of being that it did not know it could ever achieve.

THOMAS MERTON

25

We need to rediscover how to give form to our most urgent feelings, aspirations and fears, so that we may understand ourselves better through movement, color, rhythm, music, ritual and ceremonial; in our creation of a home, of a garden.

JAMES ROOSE-EVANS

Having time for play, making it an integral part of our life, essential to the rhythmic flow of our living, preserves a spirit of play in all we do. At the same time our spirit of play helps us to preserve a time for play in the rhythm of our life.

ANNE BRENNAN & JANICE BREWI

A detective novel, honestly and cleverly written, may draw us enticingly into such an experience of harmony; so may a poem or a statue; certainly music.

WILLIAM MCNAMARA

28

For many people starting a journal is the religious turning point of their lives.

MORTON KELSEY

29

At the inner core of music is the possibility that performing can touch and change the human heart.

JANET BAKER

30

Art makes places and opens spaces for reflection.

IRIS MURDOCH

31

Prayer and play make my living and working more Godlike.

ANNE BRENNAN & JANICE BREWI

APRIL

PRAYER IS BEING ATTENTIVE

The moments after supper were the most peaceful of the day as I sat outside the tent with a cup of coffee and let the day play back to me in memory, relishing its good moments and reliving the feelings and thoughts that had come to me. It was not a deliberate attempt to pray, but it usually became a prayer of gratitude for God's goodness.

GERARD HUGHES

Some of us hardly notice what is around us. I am a bit like that. Friends would often tease me that I passed by flowers, insects and birds and even large objects, like cows and bulls, without noticing that they were there. It was a relief the day I realized that it was alright to be like this, and that I was not alone. Strangely then I began to become more aware of what was around me and more attentive to it. A whole new world had opened up!

Just as we can be inattentive to the world outside of us, so we can be equally inattentive to our inner world. We may not know that we are angry or sad or stressed, or if we are aware of discomfort, not be able to name its source. To know how to be attentive to ourselves is important.

We are so often distracted, not present to ourselves, to others, to what is around us – or to God. Attention is a wonderful thing; it connects us to what is real, to God.

Happiness is the fruit of contemplation.

WILLIAM McNAMARA

The fullness of joy is to behold God in everything.

JULIAN OF NORWICH

To discover God in the smallest and most ordinary things, as well as in the greatest, is to possess a rare and sublime faith.

JEAN-PIERRE DE CAUSSADE

Learn how to see, for to see is the beginning of wonder.

MICHAEL MAYNE

The present moment holds infinite riches, but you will only enjoy them to the extent of your faith and love. The more a soul loves, the more it longs; the more it hopes, the more it finds.

JEAN-PIERRE DE CAUSSADE

Taking a long loving look at a cherry, delighting in its roundness and redness, is as important as eating it.

WILLIAM MCNAMARA

Listening to God is not about newness, but about nowness.

JOYCE HUGGETT

Absolute attention is prayer.

SIMONE WEIL

9

A saint is one who walks when he walks, who talks when he talks, who does not dream while listening, who does not think while acting.

ANONYMOUS

10

To listen closely with every fibre of our being, at every moment of the day, is one of the most difficult things in the world, and yet it is essential if we mean to find the God whom we are seeking.

ESTHER DE WAAL

11

Emotional excitement makes attention impossible. It is necessary to quieten something in ourselves first.

BRIGID MARLIN

12

To be fully committed to the present moment is to find ourselves, to enter into ourselves … this being wholly conscious is an experience of unity and simplicity.

JOHN MAIN

13

To think too quickly of prayer as a matter of words can be a most discouraging thing.

ALAN ECCLESTONE

14

More and more, meditative music helped me to drop into inner stillness, which, for me, became the pre-requisite for alert, attentive and accurate listening to God.

JOYCE HUGGETT

15

A lot of "distractions" would vanish if we realized that we are not bound at all times to ignore the practical problems of our life when we are at prayer. On the contrary, sometimes these problems actually ought to be the subject of meditation.

THOMAS MERTON

16

If something keeps interrupting your prayer, spend some time talking to God about it.

ELIZABETH SETON

17

We must learn to be alert and to relax at the same time.

ANTONY OF SOUROZH

18

One way to recollect the mind easily in the time of prayer, and preserve it more in tranquility, is not to let it wander too far at other times; you should keep it strictly in the presence of God; and being accustomed to think of him often, you will find it easy to keep your mind calm at the time of prayer, or at least to recall it from its wanderings.

BROTHER LAWRENCE

We shall often be besieged by wandering and irrelevant thoughts. When that happens we must remember that we are much more than the thoughts which wander.

H A WILLIAMS

Distractions in prayer play an important role in Christian life. They show me where healing is needed in my life.

ROBERT FARICY

Meditation means remaining in the center, being rooted in the center of your own being, and contemplation is being in the temple with him. The temple is your own heart, your own center.

JOHN MAIN

Meditation is the attempt to provide the soul with a proper environment in which to grow and become.

MORTON KELSEY

Going into deeper and deeper layers of self is a very helpful exercise in self-knowledge in addition to making for good prayer … Who am I? How do I feel today? … What has been important to me? …

What did I really want to achieve, win, avoid? Overall, what am I doing with my life? Do I really want this? I find as I force myself to verbalize answers to questions like these, I am usually getting to know myself better.

JOHN POWELL

It takes time to think. It takes time to become conscious.

SCOTT PECK

25

Contemplate what lies before you. It is God's way of making himself present.

CARLO CARRETTO

26

Contemplative prayer can be looked at as a lifestyle … a lifestyle dedicated to maximum awareness. Those who adopt it – contemplatives – desire to become as conscious as they can possibly be.

Scott Peck

27

Just being aware is a holy place.

Dorin Barter

28

No observation without gladness.

St Bonaventure

29

And now, here is my secret, a very simple secret: it is only with the heart that one can see rightly; what is essential is invisible to the eye … It is the time you have wasted on your rose that makes your rose so important.

ANTOINE de SAINT-EXUPERY

30

Gaze at the beauty of earth's greenings.

HILDEGARDE de BINGEN

MAY

PRAYER IS BEING QUIET

"A person often feels a need for solitude, which for him is a vital necessity. The fact that he feels this vital necessity … is a sign that he has a deeper nature," wrote Soren Kierkegaard.

Silence is about depth, about deepening one's knowledge of God and of oneself. In fact, the second has to come first. It is as I have the courage to meet myself in the depths of my own soul that I discover who I truly am, and that I am like God! This might seem an

astounding statement, but the way the saint and mystic St. Catherine of Genoa put it is: "My me is God nor do I know my selfhood save in him." This is knowledge that comes from the heart not the head, and from the "prayer of the heart" that grows in the silence.

This kind of praying requires discipline and time. We should not be daunted; we can make a start. We can accustom ourselves more to silence, build in times of silence. We can turn off the radio or television for a period and decide that we will go about some task quietly. We can seek out quiet places to visit. Now and again we can stop and be aware of the silence, listen to it – for it speaks. We can find out if there is a prayer group nearby that is exploring quiet or meditative prayer. Then as the desire grows, it will be the right time to take further steps – a retreat perhaps.

Nothing in all creation is so like God as stillness.

MEISTER ECKHART

Be silent, and listen to God… Let all within you listen to him. This silence of all outward and earthly affection and of human thoughts within us is essential if we are to hear his voice.

FRANÇOIS FENELON

Be still
Listen to the stones of the wall.
Be silent, they try
To speak your
Name.

THOMAS MERTON

My house being now all stilled.

JOHN OF THE CROSS

Very early the next morning, long before daylight, Jesus got up and left the house. He went out of the town to a lonely place, where he prayed.

MARK 1:35 (GNB)

Unless one takes time to turn inward and be silent, meditation and spiritual quest will not get very far.

THOMAS KELSEY

In stillness we learn to remain with the energy that arises from the contact we have made with our own spiritual nature.

JOHN MAIN

This kind of silence cannot be hurried or forced; it does not come through effort. Instead, it must be allowed to happen.

MORTON KELSEY

Life is meant to be lived from a Center, a divine Center.

THOMAS KELLY

Through the use of silence, we not only drive out our desire to dominate and control but also learn to listen to one another.

LECHMAN

It takes daily courage to expose oneself to God's word and to allow oneself to be judged by it … What shall we do, in order to penetrate into this silence before God? … Not one of us lives such a hectic life that he cannot spare the time … to be still and let the silence gather … to stand in the presence of eternity and to let it speak, to enquire from it about our condition, and to gaze deep into himself and far out, beyond and above … to know the eternal quiet which rests in God's love.

DIETRICH BONHOEFFER

12

Be still and know that I am God.

PSALM 46:10

13

When we try to compose ourselves, unrest redoubles in intensity, not unlike the manner in which at night, when we try to sleep, cares or desires assail us with a force that they do not possess during the day … if at first we achieve no more than the understanding of how much we lack in inner unity, something will have been gained, for in some way we will have made contact with that center.

ROMANO GUARDINI

14

Do not think you will ever attain the prayer of quiet by dint of your own efforts … simply and humbly say: thy will be done.

TERESA OF AVILA

15

Just sit down and relax.

JAMES BORST

16

The aim of silence is the perceiving of what will be offered to us, of the word that will resound in the silence.

ANTHONY BLOOM

17

The prayer of silence has an active and social as well as a religious and personal value. In it the soul feeds upon God, draws new vitality from the source of all life. The citizen who is so strengthened is worth more to the state than the one whose roots do not strike deep into eternity.

EVELYN UNDERHILL

18

What is here urged are inward practices of the mind at the deepest levels, letting it swing like the needle, to the polestar of the soul.

THOMAS KELLY

19

Silence can open a door on a new dimension of reality… Where there seemed to be only an endless, gray alley of concrete and mortar, or a prison of velvet walls with scarcely air to breathe, in silence we find ourselves in open country.

MORTON KELSEY

20

We cannot live well unless there is something in our lives which offers us from time to time the possibility of absolute detachment and solitude.

WILLIAM ERNEST HOCKING

21

The silence of the Christian is a listening silence.

DIETRICH BONHOEFFER

22

What is sought is … worship undergirding every moment, living prayer, the continuous current and background to all moments of life.

THOMAS KELLY

23

A person often feels a need for solitude, which for him is a vital necessity. The fact that he feels this vital necessity … is a sign that he has a deeper nature.

SOREN KIERKEGAARD

24

I find that I need a couple of hours each week … to see what I have been doing, how I have been doing, and what I need to be doing … a time for centering.

MORTON KELSEY

25

It is in deep solitude that I find the gentleness with which I can truly love.

THOMAS MERTON

26

God is the still point at the center.

JULIAN OF NORWICH

27

Pure stillness, silence are not inactive. They are harmonized energy, energy that has reached its highest and destined goal, and in this harmony the power and meaning of all movement is contained.

JOHN MAIN

In this temple of God, in this the divine dwelling place, God alone rejoices with the soul in the deepest silence. There is no reason for the intellect to stir or seek anything, for the Lord who created it wishes to give it repose there.

TERESA OF AVILA

Only the silent hear.

MOTHER MARY CLARE

But I have stilled and quieted my soul;
like a weaned child with its mother,
like a weaned child is my soul within me.

PSALM 131:2

31

Silence is the matrix of eternity.

MOTHER MARY CLARE

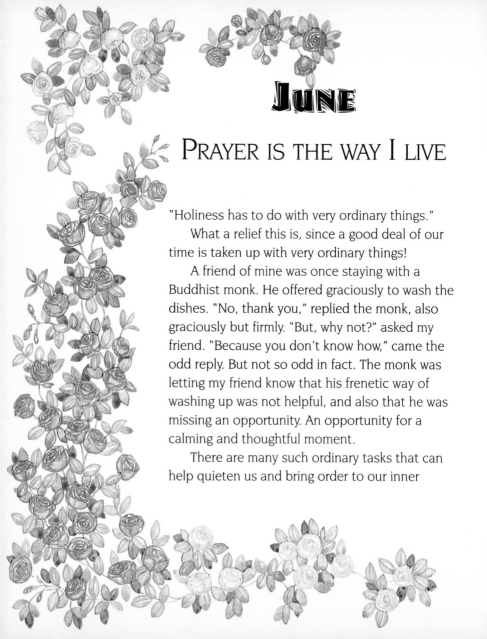

June

Prayer is the Way I Live

"Holiness has to do with very ordinary things."

What a relief this is, since a good deal of our time is taken up with very ordinary things!

A friend of mine was once staying with a Buddhist monk. He offered graciously to wash the dishes. "No, thank you," replied the monk, also graciously but firmly. "But, why not?" asked my friend. "Because you don't know how," came the odd reply. But not so odd in fact. The monk was letting my friend know that his frenetic way of washing up was not helpful, and also that he was missing an opportunity. An opportunity for a calming and thoughtful moment.

There are many such ordinary tasks that can help quieten us and bring order to our inner selves as well as our outer. That is, if they are done calmly and with time enough to enjoy the task and the moment.

What are some ordinary tasks you could approach this way?

Holiness has to do with very ordinary things.

RUTH BURROWS

The problem is that our spirituality is split: we have split God off from life.

GERARD HUGHES

The Lord's Prayer is not only a prayer, but a whole way of life expressed in the form of a prayer.

ANTHONY OF SOUROZH

The time of business does not with me differ from the time of prayer and in the noise and clatter of my kitchen, while several persons are at the same time calling for different things, I possess God in as great tranquility as if I were upon my knees at the blessed sacrament.

BROTHER LAWRENCE

We need to enter each day with a naked confidence. God will not give us more than we can bear.

TILDEN EDWARDS

An in-depth experience of life deliberately lived and not just managed – that's the solid stuff of mysticism. It involves pain and pleasure, prose and poetry, doctrine and insight, work and play, sorrow and joy – the whole mystery of life.

WILLIAM MCNAMARA

Faith does not hide difficulties or belittle them. "Without being weakened in faith Abraham considered …" Let us not fear to consider what we are up against.

AMY CARMICHAEL

Life is difficult.
This is a great truth, one of the greatest truths. It is a great truth because once we truly see this truth, we transcend it. Once we know that life is difficult – once we truly understand and accept it – then life is no longer difficult. Because once it is accepted, the fact that life is difficult no longer matters.

SCOTT PECK

9

It is (the) inner life that helps us order our perceptions,
shape our understanding, receive what we see and hear

MELVYN MATTHEWS

10

Contemplation and action are both necessary to basic stability.

MOTHER MARY CLARE

11

The Lord is my pace-setter, I shall not rush ... Even though I have a
great many things to accomplish each day, I will not fret.

TOKI MIYASHINA (PS. 23)

When you don't have enough time to get everything done, stop for a moment and pray. Then place your work before God as you do it. What you can't finish, leave, even if others become insistent and refuse to understand, for God has not given you this work to do.

MICHEL QUOIST

Wisdom consists in doing the next thing you have to do, doing it with your whole heart, and finding delight in doing it.

MEISTER ECKHART

In all ages, ardent and magnificent souls have thought that in order to do enough it was absolutely necessary to do too much.

LEON BLOY

15

Live without fuss.

FRANÇOIS DE SALES

16

An elder said: "The reason why we do not get anywhere is that we do not know our limits, and we are not patient in carrying on the work we have begun. But without any labor at all we want to gain possession of virtue."

DESERT FATHERS

17

In the struggle to try to understand what we know, and think about what we understand, we develop ourselves, and each person finds the truth in the only way he can – by living it!

BRIGID MARLIN

18

Make everyday life your prayer. Happy is he who in his daily life returns again and again to prayer … Those who return again and again to prayer will never be completely overcome by everyday life.

KARL RAHNER

19

It is a splendid habit to laugh inwardly at yourself. It is the best way to put oneself in a good temper and to find God again, without more ado.

ABBE DE TOURVILLE

20

Unless we learn to live care-lessly, we will be fruitlessly wasting our strength on the air.

MICHEL QUOIST

21

The true contemplative is one who has discovered the art of finding leisure even in the midst of his work, by working with such a spirit of detachment and recollection that even his work is a prayer.

THOMAS MERTON

A background yearning for God can be sustained
in a midst of any activity.

GUY BRINKSWORTH

No prayer is effectual except in so far as it is the
expression of the offering of the whole life.

J H OLDHAM

24

The whole of life is important – political, economic
and social, and none of these aspects is
untouched by religion as we understand it.

DESMOND TUTU

25

To pray is to anchor the finite will in the will of
God.

ANONYMOUS

26

Saying "Yes" to God's gift of love and life primarily
and above all else means choosing love as a life
principle.

JOHN POWELL

Without the contemplative dimension in our lives, we cannot be fully human.

MOTHER MARY CLARE

28

A way of testing whether our love of self is God-centered or self-centered is to ask of our moods and inner feelings, when we come to review the day, "on whose behalf was I happy, sad, indignant, angry, delighted, and so on, and who is benefiting from what I am doing?"

GERARD HUGHES

Wisdom and understanding are the fruits of prayer. We become clearer about the end to which we are traveling on life's pilgrimage, and more certain of the means to be adopted to get there. And however rough the going becomes we have the courage to go on remaining deep down at peace.

BASIL HUME

We should fall asleep with God in our last thoughts, with the desire that we may spend the night with him, and that, while our conscious minds take their rest, our unconscious minds may be open to his influence and teaching.

JACK WINSLOW

JULY

PRAYER IS FACING
WHAT I FEAR

"Maturity," Esther de Waal tells us "comes only by confronting what has to be confronted within ourselves."

Often we avoid praying or being still because consciously or unconsciously we fear we will come face to face with a side of ourselves we want to avoid. If we will not face this fear then we cannot grow or deepen our knowledge of God.

How do we begin to face what we fear? A simple exercise may get us started:

Sit quietly for half an hour in a quiet place and think about these questions: What are you most afraid of – about yourself? What do you most fear? What are the subjects you avoid talking about?

Write down your answers. You might want to continue this exercise another time, or share your answers with a trusted friend or spiritual advisor.

The unconscious contradictions of life … deepen contemplative prayer.

WILLIAM JOHNSTON

There needs to be in our lives some space in which we begin by prayerfully acknowledging whatever crowds in on us: anxieties about health or career; anger, jealousy, sexual needs; the faces of those we love; worries about the world – having acknowledged them before God, we need to let them fall away – repeatedly if necessary – and allow a pool of deep silence to grow within.

TERRY TASTARD

Solitude and suffering open the human mind.

IGJUGARJUK (a Caribou Eskimo solitary)

The longest journey is the journey inwards.

DAG HAMMARSKJOLD

Courage – big-heartedness – is the most essential virtue on the spiritual journey.

MATTHEW FOX

The invitations that prayer extends can be frightening. We are invited to go where we have not been before, to abandon the supports with which we have traveled the previous journey of our lives.

BARBARA METZ & JOHN BURCHILL

The desert is initially a negative encounter; it is the place where illusions are smashed, the place of stripping, of unmasking, of purgation. It is therefore inevitably a place of great pain and upheaval. It is also the place of discovery of that central solitude which exists at the core of each of us.

KENNETH LEECH

Maturity comes only by confronting what has to be confronted within ourselves.

ESTHER DE WAAL

The source of all our thinking, desiring and willing, and therefore of all our behavior, is within us. If we are unwilling to come to know this inner world, we cannot come to know ourselves and therefore we cannot know the direction of our lives. If we neglect this inner world, or we anesthetize ourselves against it in some way, we shut ourselves off from God, from the source of our freedom, and so condemn ourselves to become non-persons.

GERARD HUGHES

Behind all that we fear from our unconscious world there is a great love; a love which pours forth out of our own soul. But this love of God is so intense and so demanding that we hesitate to enter into relationship with it.

JOHN SANFORD

Our emotions are messages from God that can tell us much about our spiritual quest.

ELIZABETH SETON

God wants to know us … in total depth and reality, the darkness as well as the light, the anger as well as the love.

MORTON KELSEY

In the silence of prayer all of (our) demons will come to assail us. They will emerge from the depths of our consciousness once the surface activity of our lives has been taken away. In the silence of prayer we will have to struggle with them and, in the confidence that the darkness is in truth the darkness of love, learn how to disarm them.

MELVYN MATTHEWS

14

Prayer puts us in touch with our inner landscape, but if I only pray when the weather is favorable, that is, when I feel good about it and experience peace, assurance, happiness and confidence, then I shall learn little about the inner journey and remain imprisoned behind the bars of my unquestioning mind.

GERARD HUGHES

15

There is no such thing as failure in prayer. If I feel bored, empty, or angry when I pray, this can be as much a sign that I am in touch with God as when I feel full of peace, joy and delight in God's presence.

GERARD HUGHES

16

Hear my prayer, O Lord;
let my cry for help come to you.
Do not hide your face from me
when I am in distress.

PSALM 102:1

17

Finding the right questions is as crucial as finding the right answers.

HENRI NOUWEN

18

When you feel you have no desire for God, when your will is arid and constrained and you seem incapable of any spiritual activity, do not be upset. It is a boon, a good thing. ... God is taking you by the hand and guiding you in the dark, as we guide a blind man, along a strange road to an end you simply cannot imagine. You could never of yourself find this road or reach your journey's end.

JOHN OF THE CROSS

19

Are you in the dark just now in your circumstances, or in your life with God? Then remain quiet. If you open your mouth in the dark, you will talk in the wrong mood: darkness is the time to listen.

OSWALD CHAMBERS

A soul in trouble is near unto God.

APOCRYPHAL SAYING OF ST PETER

21

If our prayer is no more than the spiritual equivalent of talking about the weather, it is perhaps not surprising that it fails to satisfy, let alone to attract. But, if, as with any intimate human relationship, nothing is too important or too trivial to be excluded, then our feelings, our questions, our cries for help – in short our protests – will have a place within it.

GORDON MURSELL

Sometimes our prayers will have to be persevering, stubbornly persistent, in the face of apparent silence from God.

GORDON MURSELL

23

Are you my fellow travelers wrestling with sin and guilt? Be glad of that. You are not in hell; you are on a path, or want to know about a path, or believe there must be a path, which will lead to a place of goodness.

DORIN BARTER

24

Blessed are those whose strength is in you,
who have set their hearts on pilgrimage.
As they pass through the Valley of Baca,
they make it a place of springs;
the autumn rains also cover it with pools.

PSALM 84:6

25

Moreover, when suffering comes we should not become
obsessed with it.

THOMAS GREEN

26

Suffering can be creative. If your prayer is one of suffering –
just acceptance of suffering – you will find that your creativity is
wonderfully actuated.

WILLIAM JOHNSTON

27

We should be glad if we are vulnerable. It means that we can love and
are finding our truest selves where God is.

H A WILLIAMS

28

There is no end to the tearing up of roots that is involved on our journey.

TEILHARD DE CHARDIN

29

Who shall separate us from the love of Christ?

ROMANS 8:35

30

Holy are you,
you that cleanse deep hurt.

HILDEGARDE DE BINGEN

31

He loves us and delights in us, and so he wills us to love him and delight in him and trust mightily in him, and all shall be well … you will see it for yourself, that every kind of thing shall be well.

JULIAN OF NORWICH

August

Prayer is growing up

I have a framed poster hanging in my study. It says: "Everybody wants to be someone, but not everybody wants to grow." The words are Goethe's – words that struck me forcibly the first time I read them.

Growing is a delicate business. Like plants and flowers we need the right conditions, but we don't need to be perpetually digging up the ground to see what growth is taking place. Such continual introspection kills growth.

What is happening will become evident in time; we will realize it when we least expect it.

Being gentle with ourselves is the advice most often given by spiritual directors.

On the other hand to want to grow, to learn from life's circumstances, to become more fully ourselves, and more Godlike, is essential. We are continually faced with the choice of staying just as we are or opening ourselves up to be changed – in our actions, our moods and our habits.

What is needed to make progress? "Only determination" we are told by Serapham of Sarov. The determination to grow up.

The call of Jesus is a call to maturity.

JOHN MAIN

I feel quite different from last year: but in ways rather difficult to define. Deeper in. More steady on my knees though not yet very steady on my feet. Not so rushing up and down between blankness and vehement consolations. Still much oscillation, but a kind of steady line persists instead of zigzags.

EVELYN UNDERHILL

There are natural turning-points, crossroads or periods of crisis when the human psyche demands a conversion in its process of growth.

WILLIAM JOHNSTON

Growth of the human person takes place in the dark.

MATTHEW FOX

Turn then to your inner mirror, which if you persist will show you all you need to know. It is not an easy road; but as long as you tread it, you will be in a state of grace.

BRIGID MARLIN

It is important to learn to see meditation as a way of growth, a way of deepening our own commitment to life, and so a way leading to our own maturity.

JOHN MAIN

Allow him to call you as you are – with all your faults of personality as well as good points – and know that he does not force you into ways of praying and response that are not fully growth points for you as you now are.

DONAL NEARY & DERMOT KING

God is making us spell out our own souls. It is slow work, so slow that it takes God all time and eternity to make a man and woman after His own purpose. The only way we can be of use to God is to let Him take us through the nooks and crannies of our own characters. It is astounding how ignorant we are about ourselves! ... How many of us have learned to look in with courage?

OSWALD CHAMBERS

God is working on you in order that you may no longer be a child, tossed about by every wind, a prey to external influences. He has given you your own grace, your own nature (in so far as it is good), your own distinctive character. You are therefore required to be yourself and not anyone else.

ABBE DE TOURVILLE

It is an important skill of wisdom to be able to distinguish the true self from the false self in one's daily flux of moods: and it has immense bearing on the questions of options for or against faith.

M P GALLAGHER

Everything – success or failure, great or small – contains within itself an opportunity for growth.

GERARD HUGHES

(A person) is able to determine himself through decisions made in the center of his being.

PAUL TILLICH

Prayer, descending into the depths of God, is not there to make life easy for us. Prayer: not for any kind of result, but in order to create with Christ a communion in which we are free.

BROTHER ROGER

St. Seraphim of Sarov, when asked what it was that made some people remain sinners and never make any progress while others were becoming saints and living in God, answered: "Only determination."

ANTHONY OF SOUROZH

You ask yourself, "Have I prayed well today?" Do not try to find out how deep your emotions were, or how much deeper you understand things divine; ask yourself: "Am I doing God's will better than I did before?" If you are, prayer has brought its fruits, if you are not, it has not, whatever amount of understanding or feeling you may have derived from the time spent in the presence of God.

THEOPHANE THE RECLUSE

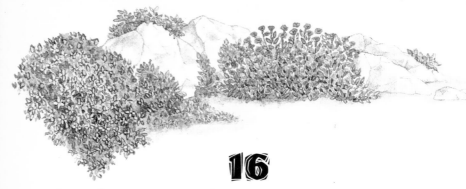

16

If we really want to pray, we have to give time to learning its lessons.

MOTHER MARY CLARE

17

Victory and growth need constant affirmation, constant development, reintegration. The growth available is like an endless spiral staircase. If one stops climbing, where is there to go?

MORTON KELSEY

18

Listen to your life. See it for the fathomless mystery that it is. In the boredom and the pain of it no less than in the excitement and gladness: touch, taste, smell your way to the heavenly and hidden heart of it because, in the last analysis, all moments are key moments, and life itself is grace.

FREDERICK BUECHNER

I do not doubt you have got on substantially during this last year, especially your General Notes make me think so. This means that we must not make any radical or very tangible changes … A gentle general horror of self and a simple flight away from self to God and Christ … this will brace you finely.

BARON VON HUGEL

A person may travel through labyrinthine paths to reach the land of wholeness.

CHRISTOPHER BRYANT

To be fully alive
to be holy,
one needs discipline,
artistry
and a little foolishness.

RABBI ABRAHAM HESCHEL

Remain a little person. By this I mean: to remain small in my own estimate of myself, to be unimportant whatever position I hold or the talents I have. It is to remember that only one thing matters, and that is what God thinks about me. Smile at yourself, your failures, at your spiritual incompetence. Have a sense of humor.

BASIL HUME

God's plan has been that human beings should come out of themselves and grow into the fulness of life in the sunlight of God's friendship. The whole process of growth was to be outward, skyward, into freedom and joy, with much laughter along the way,

CHRISTOPHER COELHO

Prayer is the articulated expression of our whole lives.

JOCK DALRYMPLE

Not that God grows through our praises, but that we do.

ST AUGUSTINE

We need beauty around us to grow.

CHRISTOPHER COELHO

Beauty has to do with seeing all life as a blessing, with returning blessing for blessing, with forging blessing of pain and suffering and tragedy and loss. Beauty needs to be made and remade. It is the vital work of the artist within ourselves.

DORIN BARTER

28

Love is the desire of every creature to find its proper place,
to find its true home.

ALAN JONES

29

Another way of approaching the tension between praying and action
is to think in terms of leisure and work. To think of opportunities for
leisure as opportunities for contemplation is to enrich the
possibilities of ordinary Christian living.

MOTHER MARY CLARE

30

Age brings wisdom for those who are open to growth.

THOMAS GREEN

31

God does not keep on beginning over and over again: He begins,
He continues and He completes.

ABBE DE TOURVILLE

September

Prayer is cooperation with God

I had not seen a newspaper for several days. I asked a person
attending the same conference whether he had one,
and explained that to read a newspaper or watch
the news on television was a daily discipline for
me, an essential part of daily prayer. He
looked surprised.
This is God's world and he is
concerned at all that

happens in it. He is working for the good of all persons everywhere and to bring about a just peace in all places of conflict. That is a task that he shares with us; it is through us that he works.

Our action, if it is truly to be a sharing in God's action, will flow from our inner being, who we are. That which moves me to pray, that which engages my imagination and my will, and that to which I am drawn and which utilizes my gifts will be an indication to me of how I can best act.

This kind of action is not easy; there is joy but also pain. This too is prayer.

Meet the world with the fulness of your being and you shall meet God.

MARTIN BUBER

As I am changed by what I discover in prayer of the love of God, so my ability to live and proclaim the nature of the Kingdom is changed.

CHARLES ELLIOTT

My soul does not find itself unless it acts.

THOMAS MERTON

In our time the road to holiness passes through the world of action.

DAG HAMMARSKJOLD

The Kingdom of God is to be conquered. It is not something which is simply given to those who leisurely, lazily, wait for it to come.

ANTHONY BLOOM

It is not so true that "prayer changes things" as that prayer changes me and I change things.

OSWALD CHAMBERS

Prayer is the necessary recommitment of ourselves to what is being done by Christ in His world, to the pain and suffering it entails no less than to the joy.

ALAN ECCLESTONE

Humankind, full of all creative possibilities, is God's work. Humankind alone is called to assist God. Humankind is called to co-create. With nature's help, humankind can set into creation all that is necessary and life-sustaining.

HILDEGARDE DE BINGEN

SEPTEMBER

9

Growth in prayer can and should give rise to cooperation, in which we use our freedom in ways big and small to draw the world to God's will.

TERRY TASTARD

Holy persons draw to themselves all that is earthly.

HILDEGARDE DE BINGEN

The coming of the Kingdom foresees a total transformation of the cosmos. That could, no doubt, be wrought by one creative act of God. It seems more likely that he prefers it to be wrought by the willing cooperation of … his people.

CHARLES ELLIOTT

Your kingdom come, your will be done.

LORD'S PRAYER

The Holy Spirit will either control your actions or cease to govern your prayers.

PERE GROU

The deepest prayer, at its nub, is a perpetual surrender to God.

THOMAS MERTON

15

Prayer, which is the fruit of true conversion, is an activity, an adventure, and sometimes a dangerous one, since there are occasions when it brings neither peace nor comfort, but challenge, conflict and new responsibility.

MOTHER MARY CLARE

16

The call of God is essentially expressive of His nature; service is the outcome of what is fitted to my nature.

OSWALD CHAMBERS

17

If prayer does not drive us out into some concrete involvement at the point of the world's need, then we must question prayer.

ELIZABETH O'CONNOR

18

Prayer … makes enemies into friends … Fervent prayer for our enemies is a great obstacle to war and the feelings that lead to it.

JIM WALLIS

19

All nature is at the disposal of
humankind.
We are to work with it.
Without it we cannot survive.

HILDEGARDE DE BINGEN

20

In solitude, in the depth's of (our) own aloneness lie the resources
for resistance to injustice.

THOMAS MERTON

21

In true prayer there is a preparedness to cooperate with God, who is
always seeking to draw the world towards his perfection. Prayer
implies cooperation, and cooperation demands an alertness about
what is going on in the world.

TERRY TASTARD

22

We should "pray the news and not just watch the news".

BILL CALLAHAN

23

Look for spiritual significance, not things men call important, big, impressive.

LESLIE WEATHERHEAD

24

I advise you first to study the modern world … Develop a sense of injustice wherever it is, but particularly in your own household.

WILLIAM JOHNSTON

25

The goal of this quest is earth healing, a healed relationship between men and women, between classes and nations, and between humans and the earth.

ROSEMARY RADFORD REUTHER

26

In the struggle for the voice of the voiceless to be heard, for the liberation of every person, the Christian finds his place – in the very front line.

BROTHER ROGER

Prayer for the Kingdom is a matter of taking sides; of committing our spiritual energies on the side of the poor against the forces of evil.

CHARLES ELLIOTT

Blessed are those who hunger and thirst for righteousness, for they will be filled.

MATTHEW 5: 6

True Christian worship can never let us be indifferent to the needs of others, to the cries of the hungry, of the naked and homeless, of the sick and the prisoner, of the oppressed and the disadvantaged.

DESMOND TUTU

The guarantee of one's prayer is not in saying a lot of words.
The guarantee of one's petition is very easy to know:

    How do I treat the poor?

    … because that is where God is.

OSCAR ROMERO

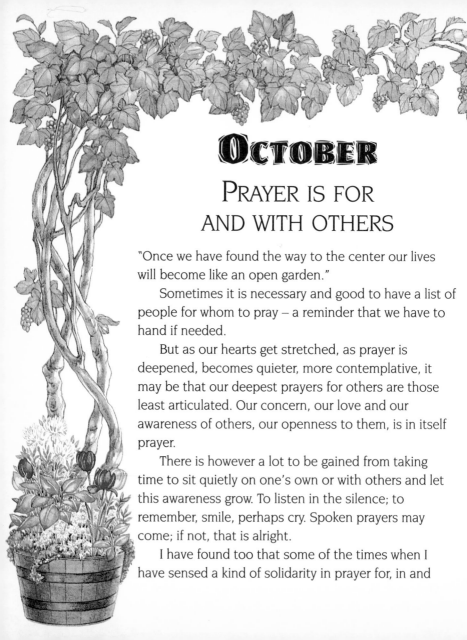

October

Prayer is for and with others

"Once we have found the way to the center our lives will become like an open garden."

Sometimes it is necessary and good to have a list of people for whom to pray – a reminder that we have to hand if needed.

But as our hearts get stretched, as prayer is deepened, becomes quieter, more contemplative, it may be that our deepest prayers for others are those least articulated. Our concern, our love and our awareness of others, our openness to them, is in itself prayer.

There is however a lot to be gained from taking time to sit quietly on one's own or with others and let this awareness grow. To listen in the silence; to remember, smile, perhaps cry. Spoken prayers may come; if not, that is alright.

I have found too that some of the times when I have sensed a kind of solidarity in prayer for, in and

with others have been odd moments at a bus stop or in a queue. This has come from using the time to become aware of where I am and of those around me, and then seeing what associations arise and letting prayer flow from that. Just waiting, whether in a car or on foot, can be immensely irritating, but can be turned into an opportunity for contemplation.

Try it the next time you find yourself in a similar situation.

I am part and parcel of the whole, and I cannot find God apart from the rest of humanity.

MAHATMA GANDHI

The inner life, the journey of the spirit, the life of prayer, is not self-enclosed like a garden created only for one's own delight. Once we have found the way to the center our lives will become like an open garden.

JAMES ROOSE-EVANS

All things are interdependent.

MEISTER ECKHART

4

One never prays apart from anyone.

CHARLES PEGUY

5

Prayer is opening into love.

TILDEN EDWARDS

6

Someday after we have mastered the winds, the waves, the tides and gravity, we will harness for God the energies of love, and then, for the second time in the history of the world, humankind will have discovered fire.

TEILHARD DE CHARDIN

Love your neighbor. You cannot really know whether you love God; but you can have some idea of whether or not you love your neighbor.

MOTHER TERESA

The result of a perfected life of prayer is "a wide-spreading love to all in common".

JAN RUYSBROECK

Nothing is really ours until we share it.

C S LEWIS

All human souls are interconnected … we can not only pray for each other, but suffer for each other.

VON HUGEL

In the encounter with one's own depth, a person comes to know, in images, the realities in that inner world that all human beings share.

MORTON KELSEY

Carry each other's burdens, and in this way you will fulfil the law of Christ.

GALATIANS 6:2

Our lives no longer belong to us alone; they belong to all those who need us desperately.

ELIE WIESEL

The essence of prayer is to hear the voice of another, of Christ, but likewise to hear the voice of each person I meet in whom Christ also addresses mine. His voice comes to me in every human voice, and his face is infinitely varied.

CATHERINE DE HUECK DOHERTY

We are called to explore the depths in ourselves, in other people and in the whole of our society, and in discovering them we need to see that these are not separate depths.

MOTHER MARY CLARE

The journey to our own heart is a journey into every heart.

JOHN MAIN

Intercession means that we rouse ourselves up to get the mind of
Christ about the one for whom we pray … It is not that we bring God
into touch with our minds, but that we rouse ourselves until God is
able to convey his mind to us about the one for whom we intercede.

OSWALD CHAMBERS

The true growth of the kingdom of God on earth depends not upon
giving but upon the life of exchange.

DORIN BARTER

Listening is perhaps the greatest service we can do for one another, and this kind of listening, as you will discover, soon begins to affect your own way of praying.

GERARD HUGHES

Being present is what counts.

JAMES ROOSE-EVANS

21

Understanding is the root.

HILDEGARDE DE BINGEN

Another name for loving from within is compassion – suffering with – which is a very great word; it is perhaps the most awful, absolute and significant of all the names of God … (and) the most intense name for the unity of men and women.

CHARLES WILLIAMS

He who prays searches not only in his own heart but he plunges deep into the heart of the whole world in order to listen more intently to the deepest and most neglected voices that proceed from its inner depths.

THOMAS MERTON

We must keep our own desire to pray, and the quality of our prayer, in relation to the larger issues around us.

MOTHER MARY CLARE

I urge, then, first of all, that requests, prayers, intercessions and thanksgiving be made for everyone – for all those who are in authority, that we may live peaceful and quiet lives in all godliness and holiness.

1 TIMOTHY 2:1-2

In intercession we begin to realize that we are not alone, that in fact we are in living and active communion with all people living and departed.

H A WILLIAMS

Real prayer leads to action, leads to our doing what we can for people. But it also saves us from fantasies of omnipotence, of imagining that we can do for people what we manifestly can't do, and from the anxiety and guilt-feelings such fantasies evoke.

H A WILLIAMS

28

We are continually borne by others. Therefore, willingly or unwillingly, we are perpetually in debt to God and to the whole creation.

MARY SHIDELER

29

In intercession we pray for the sake of others, not for ourselves. But our intercession inevitably rebounds on us. It rebounds in two chief ways which are mysteriously intertwined – in pain and in joy.

H A WILLIAMS

30

At every point in time and space where pain has its kingdom, there also are the tears of God, and sooner or later through the tears the soul of the world is renewed.

GERALD VANN

31

Behold, I will create new heavens and a new earth.

ISAIAH 65:17

November

Prayer is my heart's cry

There is a time on the inner journey when the realization comes that our deepest desire for fulfilment is met not in the things we thought so important, but in small everyday things that we may have taken for granted. Perhaps it is a view from a window, a scent, a good laugh or the faint stirring of wind rustling leaves. And we feel deep down a warmth, a wonder, a contentment. The moment passes but the memory stays. And we wonder why restlessly we seek fulfilment still in the other, the more grandiose, the "so important" to us.

It may be that the same inner

warming comes while we are praying. Or at some other time a word or prayer comes suddenly to mind. William Johnston writes about the "short word that pierces heaven". When this happens we are reminded that prayer in the deepest part of our beings never ceases, and this is reassuring. What we can also do at such times is "hold the moment", stop and be, not rush on. Or we can note that word and consciously from time to time during the day return to it in our minds. In these ways we can help bring ourselves back "into a unity" – union with God.

Prayer is only the body of the bird – desires are its wings.

JEREMY TAYLOR

Sanctity does not destroy human desire, but builds on it.

CAROLE MARIE KELLY

If you do not hope, you will not find what is beyond your hopes.

CLEMENT OF ALEXANDRIA

Prayer is not asking. It is a longing of the soul. … It is better in prayer to have a heart without words than words without a heart.

MAHATMA GANDHI

When the soul shares the purpose of God, not coldly, but with eager desire, then there is a new fact in the spiritual world. A new way is opened whereby the Lord can enter into the hearts of men.

J H OLDHAM

Though we travel the world over to find the beautiful, we must carry it with us or we find it not.

RALPH WALDO EMERSON

God has called us to a share in his creative power, and our desire is an element in the creation of the world of tomorrow.

J H OLDHAM

Thou shalt no larger be than thy desire.

JOHN MILTON

A movement of delight, a reach of the soul towards beauty, brings the human person back into a unity with itself.

MELVYN MATTHEWS

10

One must look with the heart.

ANTOINE DE SAINT-EXUPERY

11

There is something in each one of us which drives us on to search … What it is that we seek we do not always know.

BASIL HUME

Desire is essentially an innate emptiness deep within us which craves to be filled, and can ultimately be filled only with God.

CAROLE MARIE KELLY

O God, you are my God,
earnestly I seek you;
my soul thirsts for you,
my body longs for you,
in a dry and weary land
where there is no water.

PSALM 63:1

14

I need to dwell on certain experiences of God … These experiences are foretastes of something that will be mine one day, hints of realities that cannot be known through my senses but are nevertheless true.

BASIL HUME

We can only know through our suffering and our actions what experience has taught us. It is the breath of the Holy Spirit whispering the words of life to the heart, and everything we say to others must come from this source.

JEAN-PIERRE DE CAUSSADE

Those who have made the prayer of the heart a daily practice come to experience it as a simple, yet beautiful way to their true home. It gradually leads us away from the house of fear and moves us closer to the house of love, God's house.

HENRI NOUWEN

It sometimes happens that people have a favorite phrase or word … to which they frequently return… This word has not been given them from outside but has arisen spontaneously in their hearts, and for them it is very precious. The word may be "God" or "Love" or "Peace" or "Joy" … their whole life centers around this word which keeps resounding within, even in the midst of a busy life.

WILLIAM JOHNSTON

For mental prayer – praying in words or using thoughts about God – we can make rules. There are many "methods of mental prayer", but for the prayer of the heart there is no technique, no rules.

LAURENCE FREEMAN

Prayer is as various as life. There is prayer that is swift, brief – a look, a thought; there is the long-drawn prayer of long tension; the prayer whose instant first answer is peace; the prayer that is just the pouring out of the heart – "Lord, all my desire is before thee." And as to that desire, love does not need to explain itself to love.

AMY CARMICHAEL

We pray when we ask, plead, search, yearn for what we do not know out of what we know.

MELVYN MATTHEWS

My children, your hearts are small, but prayer enlarges them and renders them capable of loving God.

CURE D'ARS

Don't imagine for a moment that your deepest aspirations can be satisfied by something outside yourself, for only the interior Master is able to fulfil your deepest needs and desires.

MICHEL QUOIST

For he satisfies the thirsty soul and fills the hungry soul with good. PSALM 107:9 (LB)

24

Labor therefore to increase the fire of thy desire.

CATHERINE OF SIENA

25

The raising of the mind to God through the desire of love.

ST BONAVENTURE

God cannot be comprehended by our intellect, or any man's – or any angel's for that matter. For both they and we are created beings. But only to our intellect is he incomprehensible, not to our love … Strike that thick cloud of unknowing with the sharp dart of longing love, and on no account whatever think of giving up.

THE CLOUD OF UNKNOWING

This is what you are to do: lift up your heart to the Lord, with a gentle stirring of love desiring him for his own sake and not for his gifts.

JOHN OF THE CROSS

He kindled your desire for himself, and bound you to him by the chain of such longing.

THE CLOUD OF UNKNOWING

As the deer pants for streams of water,
so my soul pants for you, O God.

PSALM 42:1

30

Although spiritual writers describe the various stages of prayer in ascending order, with the silent prayer of union at the top of the list, none of them implies that as we progress to higher forms of prayer, we never return to other forms. As we learn to play the piano, we begin with single notes and progress to chords, but once we have mastered the chords we do not, therefore, neglect the single melody notes. Once we have learned to play the polka, we do not avoid the waltz..Our prayer is an intricate interplay of lights and shadows, words and silence, mountain and desert.

CAROLE MARIE KELLY

December

Prayer is
becoming one with God

To experience "oneness" is essentially a gift. We can put ourselves in
the way of it, but that is all. The journey we have been making in
prayer over these months is a kind of "putting ourselves in the way of
it".

There is a purpose to this journey, and it is not only that we will
experience "the embrace of unitive love". It is that our nature
becomes transformed – that we become like God.

As such transformation progressively takes place in us and
others, so God's reign on earth becomes that much nearer. Those
that know God's embrace, embrace all that is. The world is badly in
need of such modern mystics. There are more than we might think;
this kind of journey is not just for the enclosed "religious".

All parts of the journey are essential; the different parts woven
into our daily life to make a unity. To come then to know such a unity
within oneself and beyond oneself – that is worth the journey.

Prayer unites the soul to God.

Julian of Norwich

We are all the kindred of mystics … Strange and far away from us though they seem, they are not cut off from us by some impassable abyss.

EVELYN UNDERHILL

(This) is experimental knowledge of God through the embrace of unitive love.

JEAN GERSON

4

There is an experience of being in pure consciousness which gives lasting peace to the soul. It is an experience of the Ground or Depth of being in the Center of the soul, an awareness of the mystery of being beyond sense and thought, which gives a sense of fulfilment, of finality, of absolute truth.

BEDE GRIFFITHS

5

Prayer carries us to a vision of an inner relatedness to all things.

ANNE BRENNAN & JANICE BREWI

6

We possess this unity both within ourselves and beyond ourselves as that which is the source of our life and which sustains us in being.

JAN RUYSBROECK

7

Every visible and invisible creature is a theophany or appearance of God.

JOHN SCOTUS

Prayer is not simply getting things from God, that is an initial form of prayer; prayer is getting into perfect communion with God.

OSWALD CHAMBERS

Some of the great mystics tell us that when they reach the stage of illumination they become mysteriously filled with a sense of deep reverence. Reverence of God, reverence of life in all its forms, reverence for inanimate creation too … Francis of Assisi was one such mystic. He recognized in the sun, the moon, the stars, the trees, the birds, the animals, his brothers and sisters. They were members of his family and he would talk to them lovingly. Saint Anthony of Padua went to the extent of preaching a sermon to the fish! Very foolish, of course, from our rationalist point of view. Profoundly wise … sanctifying from the mystical point of view.

ANTHONY DE MELLO

The fuller the love, the fuller the knowledge of God.

STARETZ SILOUAN

The simple vision of pure love, which is marvellously penetrating, does not stop at the outer husk of creation: it penetrates to the divinity which is hidden within.

MALAVAL

Being united to God … not in any specific manner or style, but in a thousand different ways, and the one he chooses for us is the best.

Jean-Pierre de Caussade

You have created me for yourself, and my heart is restless until it rests in you.

St Augustine

Nothing in all nature is so lovely and so vigorous, so perfectly at home in its environment as a fish in the sea. Its surroundings give to it a beauty, quality and power which is not its own. We take it out, and at once a poor, limp, dull thing, fit for nothing, is gasping away its life. So the soul sunk in God living the life of prayer, is supported, filled, transformed in beauty by a vitality and a power which are not its own.

Evelyn Underhill

15

The mystics constantly tell us, that the goal of ... prayer and of the hidden life ... is union with God ... What does union with God mean? Not a nice feeling which we enjoy in devout moments ... Union with God means such an entire self-giving to the Divine Charity, such identification with its interests, that the whole of our human nature is transformed in God, irradiated by His absolute light, His sanctifying grace ... Each time this happens it means that one more creature has achieved its destiny: and each soul in whom the life of the spirit is born, sets out towards that goal.

EVELYN UNDERHILL

16

You who long to know where your beloved is and where you may find him so as to be united with him. He dwells within you. You are yourself the tabernacle, his secret hiding place. Rejoice, exult, for all you could possibly desire, all your heart's longing is so close, so intimate as to be within you; you cannot be without him.

JOHN OF THE CROSS

That measureless love which is God himself dwells in the pure deeps of our spirit like a burning brazier of coal.

JAN RUYSBROECK

Mysticism in the proper sense is an intense realization of God within the self and the self embraced within God in vivid nearness.

MICHAEL RAMSEY

19

To pray is to descend with the mind in the heart and there to stand before the face of the Lord, ever present, all seeing, within you.

THEOPHAN THE RECLUSE

It will feel as if they had always dwelt there, united with God, although such moments are short. And yet these moments are experienced as if they were an eternity.

JOHANNES TAULER

21

We "possess" him in proportion as we realize ourselves to be possessed by him in the inmost depths of our being.

THOMAS MERTON

22

The interior law of charity and of love which is above all laws and rules and observances. That is why I have spoken of the living flame of love, the blind stirring of love, the small fire and the murmuring stream.

WILLIAM JOHNSTON

23

Enjoys a certain contact of the soul with the divinity; and it is God himself who is then felt and tasted.

JOHN OF THE CROSS

24

For the love of God is found to be a unitive love, not a love for the individual alone but a love which unites that soul to itself, to creation and to all other beings, for it is the ground of being itself.

MELVYN MATTHEWS

25

Everything beckons to us who perceive it.

RAINER MARIA RILKE

26

He is the being of all … He is thy being but thou art not his.

THE CLOUD OF UNKNOWING

27

As air is penetrated by the brightness and the heart of the sun, and iron is penetrated by fire … yet each of them keeps its own nature – the fire does not become iron, and the iron does not become fire, so likewise is God in the being of the soul … The creature never becomes God, nor does God ever become the creature.

JAN RUYSBROECK